ABRAH_ ____

VERGHESE

BIOGRAPHY

Verghese's Journey into
Medicine and Writing, His
Rise to Prominence and
How He's Shaping the
Future of Medicine

Fowler Faircloth

TABLE OF CONTENT

CHILDHOOD AND EARLY YEARS: FROM ETHIOPIA TO INDIA

Abraham Verghese's life began in the highlands of Ethiopia, where he was born to Indian parents in 1955. His father was a teacher and his mother was a nurse, and together they raised Abraham and his two younger brothers.

Growing up in Ethiopia, Verghese was exposed to a wide range of cultures and languages. He attended a British school where he learned English and was also fluent in Amharic, the local language. He spent his summers in India, where he was immersed in the rich traditions of his ancestral homeland.

In 1974, a communist military coup led to the ousting of Emperor Haile Selassie, and the Verghese family was forced to flee the country. They settled in India, where Verghese continued his education and eventually attended medical school.

Despite the upheaval of his early years, Verghese remembers his childhood fondly. He has spoken of the deep connections he formed with people from different cultures and the lasting impact those experiences had on his life and work.

In many ways, Verghese's childhood set the stage for his later achievements in medicine and writing. His multicultural upbringing gave him a unique perspective on the human experience and inspired his lifelong commitment to understanding and healing others.

As we delve deeper into Verghese's life and work, we'll see how these early experiences shaped the man he became and the legacy he is leaving behind.

VERGHESE'S JOURNEY INTO MEDICINE AND WRITING

Abraham Verghese's journey into medicine and writing is a fascinating one, full of twists and turns, successes and setbacks, and moments of both clarity and confusion. Verghese was exposed to a rich mix of cultures and languages from an early age, which no doubt helped to shape his outlook on life and his approach to both medicine and writing.

Growing up, Verghese was a voracious reader, devouring everything from classic novels to medical textbooks. His parents instilled in him a deep sense of respect for education and hard work, and he took these lessons to heart, excelling in school and eventually earning a scholarship to study medicine at the University of Madras in India.

It was at medical school that Verghese began to find his voice as both a doctor and a writer. Inspired by the work of the great physician-writers of the past, such as Anton Chekhov and William Carlos Williams, he began to experiment with incorporating elements of narrative storytelling into his medical practice. He found that by taking the time to listen to his patient's stories and to share his own experiences and insights with them, he was able to build deeper, more meaningful relationships with them and provide more effective, compassionate care.

As Verghese's medical career began to take off, he also began to explore his passion for writing more seriously. He published his first book, a memoir titled "My Own Country," in 1994, which chronicled his experiences as a physician treating patients with HIV/AIDS in rural Tennessee in the early 1980s. The book was a critical and commercial success, earning widespread praise for its raw, honest portrayal of the epidemic and the people it affected.

Encouraged by the response to "My Own Country," Verghese continued to write and publish throughout his career, exploring a wide range of subjects and genres, from medical memoirs and novels to essays and articles on everything from the history of medicine to the challenges facing the healthcare system today.

Along the way, he has become known not just as a great physician and writer but as a powerful advocate for humanistic medicine and a fierce critic of the forces that threaten to erode the art and science of healing.

His journey has not been without its share of setbacks and struggles. He has faced criticism from some quarters for his advocacy of humanistic medicine, with some arguing that his approach is too idealistic and impractical for today's fast-paced, profit-driven healthcare system. He has also had to grapple with personal tragedies, including the loss of his first wife to cancer and the challenges of raising a family while maintaining a demanding career.

Through it all, however, Verghese has remained steadfast in his commitment to medicine and writing and to the idea that the two can and should be intertwined. He has continued to push the boundaries of both fields, using his platform to advocate for a more compassionate, patient-centered approach to healthcare and to inspire the next generation of physician-writers to follow in his footsteps.

As we move forward into an uncertain future full of new challenges and opportunities, Verghese's journey serves as a reminder of the power of storytelling to heal, connect, and inspire. Whether we are doctors, writers, or simply people trying to make sense of our place in the world, his example shows us that by finding our own voices and sharing our own stories, we can make a difference, both in our own lives and in the lives of those around us.

THE HEALING TOUCH

Abraham Verghese's approach to medicine has been characterized as old-fashioned, holistic, and deeply personal. His philosophy of healing revolves around the idea that every patient is unique and that effective treatment requires a close and empathetic relationship between the physician and the patient.

Verghese's commitment to the traditional art of physical examination sets him apart from many of his contemporaries. He has spoken extensively about the importance of a thorough physical exam, which he believes can reveal much more about a patient than any diagnostic test. For Verghese, the exam is a ritual of sorts, a way of honoring the patient and acknowledging their humanity.

Verghese's approach to medicine is rooted in the belief that a doctor must have an intimate understanding of the patient's life and circumstances in order to provide the best possible care. This includes not only their medical history and symptoms but also their social and cultural background, their hopes and fears, and their spiritual beliefs.

One of the most prominent examples of Verghese's holistic approach to medicine is his work with patients suffering from HIV and AIDS. In the early days of the epidemic, when many healthcare providers were afraid to treat these patients, Verghese was on the front lines, working tirelessly to help them.

Verghese understood that effective treatment of HIV and AIDS required not only medical expertise but also compassion and empathy. He made it a point to get to know his patients on a personal level, to understand their fears and anxieties, and to provide emotional support along with medical treatment.

Verghese's philosophy of healing extends beyond the individual patient to the broader community as well. He has spoken extensively about the importance of community-based care, arguing that the best way to improve health outcomes is to invest in local clinics and hospitals.

For Verghese, community-based care is not only more effective but also more ethical. It allows patients to receive care in a familiar and supportive environment, surrounded by family and friends. It also fosters a sense of responsibility and accountability among healthcare providers, who are more likely to take a holistic and personalized approach to patient care when they are part of a tight-knit community.

Verghese's commitment to patient-centered care has earned him widespread recognition and praise. In 2015, he was awarded the National Humanities Medal by President Barack Obama for his "humanistic approach to medicine that has transformed the way doctors and patients communicate." The award recognized Verghese's efforts to promote empathy and compassion in healthcare and his belief in the power of the physical exam to connect physicians with their patients.

Despite the accolades, Verghese remains humble and dedicated to his patients. He continues to practice medicine and teach at Stanford, where he inspires a new generation of doctors to approach healthcare with empathy and compassion.

Verghese's approach to medicine serves as a powerful reminder of the importance of the human touch in healthcare. In a world where technology and specialization often take center stage, Verghese's work is a testament to the enduring power of the doctor-patient relationship and the healing power of empathy and compassion.

BREAKING INTO THE BIG LEAGUES

After completing his residency at Boston City Hospital, Verghese spent a few years working as a general practitioner in rural Tennessee. He found that his medical training had not fully prepared him for the challenges of practicing medicine in a low-resource setting. Verghese learned to rely on his instincts and experience, as well as his empathy for his patients. He also became more attuned to the social and economic factors that affect health outcomes.

In 1985, Verghese was recruited to be the chief of infectious diseases at Texas Tech University Health Sciences Center in El Paso. This was a significant turning point in his career. He moved his family to the border town, which was facing a public health crisis due to the influx of migrants from Mexico and Central America. Verghese was determined to make a difference.

At Texas Tech, Verghese became a prolific researcher and writer. He published numerous papers on infectious diseases, and he also began to write essays and stories about his experiences as a doctor. Verghese's writing gained a following, and he was soon invited to speak at medical conferences around the world.

In 1991, Verghese published his first book, "The Tennis Partner: A Story of Friendship and Loss." The book was a memoir about his friendship with a medical student who struggled with addiction.

It was also a reflection on the challenges that doctors face when caring for patients who are dealing with addiction and mental illness. The book received critical acclaim and was a commercial success.

Verghese's success as a writer helped him to become a prominent voice in the medical community. He was invited to be a guest on talk shows and to contribute articles to prestigious medical journals. He was also recruited to be a professor of medicine at Stanford University in California.

At Stanford, Verghese continued to write and practice medicine. He was particularly interested in the intersection of medicine and literature, and he taught a course on the subject. He also continued to publish articles and essays, and he wrote two more books: "My Own Country: A Doctor's Story of a Town and Its People in the Age of AIDS" and "Cutting for Stone," a novel that was based in part on his experiences working as a surgeon in Ethiopia.

"Cutting for Stone" was published in 2009 and became a bestseller. The novel was praised for its vivid depiction of life in Ethiopia and its exploration of the human condition. Verghese's ability to seamlessly integrate medical knowledge and storytelling in his writing has made him a unique and respected voice in both fields.

Verghese's rise to prominence was not without its challenges. He faced criticism from some in the medical community for his writing and his views on the importance of empathy in medicine. He was also accused of promoting a "romantic" view of medicine that was not rooted in reality. However, Verghese remained steadfast in his beliefs and continued to advocate for a more compassionate and humanistic approach to medicine.

Today, Verghese is recognized as one of the most important voices in medicine and literature. He has received numerous awards and honors, including the National Humanities Medal and the Heinz Award in the Arts and Humanities. Verghese continues to write and practice medicine, and he remains a passionate advocate for the importance of empathy and humanism in healthcare.

PERSONAL LIFE: ABRAHAM VERGHESE'S FAMILY AND HOBBIES

In this chapter, we explore the personal life of Abraham Verghese, the man behind the medical profession and writing. As we delve into his personal life, we gain insight into the family man and the things that he enjoys doing outside of his work.

Verghese has been married to Sylvia for about 11 years. The couple met in India while he was a medical student at Madras Medical College and she was a microbiology student. They have a son named Tristan. Verghese also has two other children from his first marriage namely Steven and Jacob.

In his memoir, "The Tennis Partner," Verghese discusses the impact of his friendship with a fellow doctor, David Smith, on his personal life. Smith, who was struggling with addiction, ultimately passed away due to an overdose. Verghese's reflections on this experience offer a glimpse into his emotional depth and the impact that his friendships have had on his life.

Aside from his family and friendships, Verghese has several hobbies that he enjoys pursuing in his free time. He is an avid tennis player and has written about the game in several of his books. In fact, he has even integrated tennis into his work as a doctor. In a TED talk, Verghese discusses how he uses the game to teach medical students about the importance of touch and observation. He believes that playing tennis has helped him become a better doctor, and he encourages others to find ways to integrate their hobbies and passions into their professional lives.

In addition to tennis, Verghese is also an accomplished writer and has penned several books, including "My Own Country," "Cutting for Stone," and "The Tennis Partner." He often draws inspiration from his personal life and experiences, and many of his books explore the intersection of medicine and humanity. In his writing, Verghese is known for his vivid descriptions and his ability to capture the intricacies of the human experience.

In recent years, Verghese has become an advocate for the importance of the humanities in medicine. He believes that the study of literature, art, and history can help doctors become more empathetic and better understand their patients. Verghese has even established a center for medical humanities at the Stanford School of Medicine, which aims to integrate the humanities into medical education and practice.

Overall, Abraham Verghese's personal life reflects his deep commitment to his family, friendships, and passions. His love of tennis, writing, and the humanities all play an important role in his life and work as a doctor. By exploring this side of

Verghese, we gain a fuller understanding of the man behind the professional accomplishments.

CONTROVERSIES AND CRITICISMS

Abraham Verghese's unique approach to medicine has gained him both admirers and detractors over the years. While he has been lauded for his patient-centered care and focus on the physical exam, he has also been criticized for his controversial opinions on topics ranging from electronic health records to the role of empathy in medicine.

Verghese has been a vocal critic of electronic health records (EHRs), which he believes have led to a loss of personal connection between doctors and patients. In his opinion, EHRs have made it too easy for doctors to focus on the screen instead of the person in front of them, leading to a decline in the quality of care.

While some doctors agree with Verghese's stance on EHRs, others argue that electronic records have actually improved patient care by making it easier to access medical histories and communicate with other healthcare providers. They also point out that EHRs have become a necessary tool for healthcare providers, as they are now required by law to use them.

Another topic on which Verghese has been outspoken is the role of empathy in medicine. He has argued that empathy is an essential component of good medical care, as it allows doctors to understand their patients' experiences and provide more effective treatment.

However, some critics have accused Verghese of placing too much emphasis on empathy at the expense of scientific evidence. They argue that empathy alone is not enough to ensure good medical care and that doctors must also rely on empirical research and clinical experience to make sound medical decisions.

Despite these controversies, Verghese's commitment to patient-centered care has earned him a dedicated following among both patients and medical professionals. His emphasis on the importance of the physical exam, for example, has been praised for its ability to provide a more accurate diagnosis than relying solely on technology.

Verghese has also been a strong advocate for the humanities in medicine, arguing that reading literature and exploring the arts can help doctors develop greater empathy and understanding of their patient's experiences. He has even incorporated literature into his medical training programs, using books and stories to help medical students learn about the human side of medicine.

In addition to his work as a doctor, Verghese has also been involved in several medical controversies outside of his clinical practice. He has been a vocal critic of the pharmaceutical industry, arguing that it has become too focused on profits at the expense of patient care.

Verghese has also taken a strong stance on the opioid epidemic, which he believes is fueled in part by the overprescription of pain medication. He has called for more responsible prescribing practices and greater emphasis on non-pharmacological pain management techniques.

Despite the controversies surrounding Verghese's opinions and activism, it is clear that he is deeply committed to improving patient care and advancing the field of medicine. His dedication to the physical exam and patient-centered care has helped to change the way doctors think about their role in healthcare, and his advocacy for the humanities has helped to promote a more compassionate and empathetic approach to medicine.

Overall, Verghese's unique perspective on medicine and his willingness to speak out on controversial issues have made him a respected and influential figure in the medical community. While some may disagree with his opinions, there is no denying that his contributions to the field of medicine have helped to shape its future and improve the lives of countless patients.

LOOKING TO THE FUTURE: VERGHESE'S PLANS AND ASPIRATIONS

Abraham Verghese has dedicated his life to medicine and literature, but his ambitions and aspirations go beyond his current accomplishments. In this chapter, we will explore Verghese's plans for the future and the impact he hopes to make in the medical field.

As a physician and writer, Verghese is passionate about both medicine and literature. He has been able to successfully combine these two interests throughout his career, but he believes there is still much work to be done in bridging the gap between these two fields. One of Verghese's major goals for the future is to continue to push for greater collaboration between medicine and the arts.

Verghese believes that medicine and the arts have a lot to learn from each other. For example, he believes that medical professionals could benefit from studying the narrative structure of literature to better understand their patients' experiences. In turn, he believes that writers could benefit from studying medicine to create more accurate and nuanced depictions of illness and healthcare. Verghese has already taken steps to bring these two fields together through his work as a professor at Stanford University, where he teaches courses on the intersection of medicine and the humanities.

Another major goal for Verghese is to continue his work in improving medical education. Verghese is passionate about ensuring that medical students receive a well-rounded education that goes beyond just the scientific aspects of medicine. He believes that students should be taught to view patients as people with complex stories and not just as a collection of symptoms to be diagnosed and treated.

Verghese's approach to medical education involves emphasizing the importance of the physical exam and the doctor-patient relationship. He believes that these two elements of medicine are often overlooked in modern medical education, which places a greater emphasis on technology and specialization. Verghese has been able to put this approach into practice through his work as a professor at Stanford University and through his writing.

In addition to his work in medicine and education, Verghese is also interested in the future of technology in healthcare. He believes that technology has the potential to greatly improve the efficiency and accuracy of healthcare, but he also recognizes the risks that come with relying too heavily on technology. Verghese has written extensively on this topic, exploring the ways in which technology can be used to enhance the human elements of medicine rather than replace them.

Abraham is also committed to continuing his writing career. He has already achieved great success as a writer, with several critically acclaimed books to his name. However, he believes that there is still much work to be done in the realm of medical writing. Verghese hopes to continue writing about the human side of medicine, exploring the complex relationships between doctors, patients, and their families.

Abraham's plans and aspirations for the future reflect his commitment to improving healthcare through a combination of scientific knowledge and humanistic understanding. Whether through his work as a professor, his writing, or his advocacy for greater collaboration between medicine and the arts, Verghese is committed to making a lasting impact on the world of medicine.

As we come to the end of this biography, it's clear that Abraham Verghese's life and work have left an indelible mark on the world of medicine and literature. Through his tireless dedication to his patients, his writing, and his advocacy, Verghese has made a profound impact on both the medical profession and society as a whole.

Throughout his career, Verghese has shown a deep commitment to promoting the human side of medicine. His approach is one that values not only the physical aspects of healing but also the emotional and social dimensions of care. Verghese's books, talks, and essays have highlighted the importance of patient-centered care and the need for doctors to connect with their patients on a human level.

Moreover, Verghese has been a vocal advocate for the importance of physical examination in medicine. In an era where technology has become increasingly important in healthcare, Verghese has emphasized the value of hands-on examinations and the importance of a doctor's touch in patient care. He has argued that physical examinations can provide important diagnostic clues, improve patient communication, and strengthen the doctor-patient relationship.

Verghese's legacy extends beyond the field of medicine. Through his writing, he has captured the human experience in a way that resonates with readers from all walks of life. His books explore the complexities of human relationships, the meaning of life and death, and the importance of empathy and compassion.

As a teacher and mentor, Verghese has inspired a generation of physicians and writers to follow in his footsteps. His approach to medicine, writing, and teaching has served as a model for others to emulate. He has shown us that the art of medicine and the craft of writing are intertwined and that both require a deep understanding of the human condition.

Looking to the future, Verghese's impact on medicine and literature is likely to continue to grow. As healthcare systems around the world continue to grapple with the challenges of providing patient-centered care, Verghese's message of the importance of the human touch will remain relevant. As new generations of physicians and writers emerge, they will undoubtedly look to Verghese's example as a guide and a source of inspiration.

In conclusion, Abraham Verghese is a remarkable individual who has made a profound impact on both medicine and literature. His dedication to patient-centered care, his advocacy for the importance of physical examination, and his writing have left an enduring legacy that will continue to shape the world for generations to come. Verghese's life and work serve as a testament to the power of empathy, compassion, and human connection in both medicine and life.

Printed in Great Britain
by Amazon